What Women NO About Men
What do you REALLY know about the men in your life?

By David Selley

Copyright © 2025

In **What Women NO About Men**, David Selley invites women to take a lighthearted yet honest look at the men in their lives. With wit, warmth, and just enough bite, this interactive book helps readers reflect on what really matters—kindness, honesty, humor, and more. Through scoring, stories, and the occasional rant, women are encouraged to see clearly, speak truthfully, and laugh along the way. Whether you're in love, in limbo, or somewhere in between, this book is your compass for navigating modern relationships—with clarity and comic relief.

First Edition: 2025

Other Books in the PAPA Series and Beyond:
Book 1 – *PAPA #1: The Boy in England – Growing Up Tough*
Book 2 – *PAPA #2: The Young Man in Canada – Grit, Growth & Greatness*
Book 3 – *PAPA #3: The Businessman and Entrepreneur in the USA*
Book 4 – *The Entrepreneur: Papa's Secrets #4*
Book 6 – *MARRIED FOREVER – The Four Seasons of Love*
Book 13 –GenMar – Generational Marketing Strategy – Basket to Casket Marketing 101
Book 15 – BOUNDARIES WITH BENEFITS – A Companion Journal to What Women NO

Additional books in the PAPA Series are forthcoming. See page 113 for all new titles.

No part of this publication may be reproduced, distributed, or transmitted in any form without prior written permission from the publisher, except for brief quotations used in reviews or permitted by copyright law. For permission, contact the author at davidselley08@gmail.com   This book is a work of non-fiction. Any references to real people, places, or events are intended to accurately reflect the author's experiences.

Publisher: **Promptings Publishing** - Fran Jessee has dedicated herself to bringing David Selley's PAPA Series to life. With meticulous attention to detail, Fran has edited and formatted David's Series to ensure that David's voice shines through on every page. Her commitment to preserving the authenticity of his narrative while enhancing readability makes this book a true reflection of David's experiences. For further information contact franjessee@gmail.com

Cover Design: David Selley
ISBN: 979-8-9916760-9-0
Printed in the United States of America

May You Have

May your spring bring love in bloom,
With dreams to chase and hearts in tune.
May your summer shine with endless light,
Building memories both day and night.
May your autumn teach you to embrace,
The beauty of change, the gentlest grace.
May your winter wrap you in its glow,
A love that deepens as time does flow.
Through every season, may you find,
A bond that grows, heart and mind.
Together as one, steadfast and true,
Through all of life, may love guide you..

Aloha! From beautiful Hawaii!

David Selley

Dedication

*To the brave, bold, and beautiful women who've loved,
lost, and laughed at men —
and those still trying to figure them out.*

*And to the good men...
the world needs more of you.*

— David Selley

Foreword

Let's be honest—after 87 years on this planet, I've learned a few things.

One: Men are strange.
Two: Women are extraordinary.
Three: The combination of the two makes life equal parts confusing, hilarious, and beautiful.

Now, I'm not here to give you relationship advice. Lord knows I've made enough mistakes to write another book. But I am here to offer a simple tool—a fun, eye-opening little book that might just help you sort through the nonsense and spot the truth hiding in plain sight.

What Women NO About Men isn't about blaming, shaming, or "fixing" anybody. It's about laughing, learning, and seeing clearly. Think of it as your emotional magnifying glass—with just the right amount of humor to keep it from turning into a therapy session.

Inside, you'll find ten key traits that show up—or don't—in the men you know. You'll rate them, reflect on them, maybe rant a little (go ahead, it's good for the soul). You'll probably end up knowing a lot more about the guys in your life than you did before you opened this book.

And here's my hope: that somewhere in these pages, you find clarity. Maybe even healing. And definitely a few laughs.

So grab your pen, grab a friend, and let's find out what you really "NO" about men.

With respect, a wink, and all my best wishes,

—David Selley

Introduction

10 Things Women Want —
and 1 That Changes Everything

We all have a list — even if we say we don't.

Somewhere between that second date and his third "what's for dinner?" text, we start mentally checking off traits. Some of us have actual paper lists (highlighted, underlined, and laminated). Others keep them floating in our heads — or rant about them in group chats labeled *"Emergency Only."*

We know what we want... or so we think.

Usually, it starts with the obvious:
- He's funny.
- He's cute.
- He has a job, teeth, and hopefully some form of deodorant.

But real talk? What we *look for first* isn't always what *actually matters most*.

That's why this book is built around the 10 most essential things women usually want in a man — PLUS one
bonus quality that rarely makes the first date checklist... but quietly defines the whole relationship.

The +1?

Emotional Stability.
It's not sexy until it's survival.

He could have a six-pack, recite poetry, and rescue puppies — but if he melts down every time the Wi-Fi drops? Girl, run.

So here they are:

10 things that make a man desirable...
+1 that makes him truly worth keeping.

Let's dive in. Laugh, nod, roll your eyes, and maybe cross out a few names from your past while you're at it.

Welcome to:
> ***What Women NO About Men:***
> ***What Do You REALLY Know About***
> ***the Men in Your Life?***

Disclaimer

This book contains humor, truth, and possibly emotional outbursts. Side effects may include self-awareness, fits of laughter, or relationship clarity. Use with wine and supportive friends.

Why This Book Exists

Let's be honest—women are often placed in emotional situations that make no sense.

One day you're told to "be patient," the next you're blamed for not acting sooner.

You're told to speak up, then told you're "too emotional." You want love, laughter, connection—but you're handed confusion, avoidance, and socks left on the floor.

This book won't solve every relationship problem—but it **will** help you get clear on what's actually happening in your dynamic with the men in your life.

These 10 traits are the foundation of every good (or failing) relationship. By taking time to **score**, **reflect**, and **express**, you're giving yourself permission to make clearer, more powerful decisions.

You're not crazy. You're not too much.
You just need better tools.

This book is your toolkit. Let's get to it.

A Note on the Title:
"What Women **NO** About Men"
*Yes, it's **NO**, not "know."*

In this book, **NO** isn't just a word — it's a mood, a boundary, a declaration, and occasionally... a lifestyle.

NO (noun, verb, exclamation, and full-body eye-roll): The universal sound women make when faced with mansplaining, socks on the floor, unsolicited advice, or "I didn't know you wanted help."

This title is a playful twist on what women *actually know* about men — and more importantly, what they've decided they're absolutely done with. Think of it as a celebration of wisdom earned, patience tested, and humor fully loaded.

If you're a man reading this... bless your brave soul. If you're a woman... welcome to the club.

Let's get started.

"No matter what kind of man you're dealing with, don't skip the pages. You might relate to one trait today, but every chapter holds a mirror, a giggle, or a wake-up call—because relationships, like people, are always evolving."

This book is part of David Selley's PAPA Book Series

—A 13-book collection of memoirs, relationsip wisdom, entrepreneurship and the International Entrepreneurs Assocation. As part of his Guinness World Record attempt to become the oldest author to publish the most books in one year. This series spans his journey across England, Canada and the USA. From overcoming hardships to building businesses and sustaining a 65-year marriage, these books capture the humor, resilience and wisdom of a life-well-lived.

TABLE OF CONTENTS

May You Have - A Poem iii
Dedication iv
Forward v
Introduction: 10 Things Women Want +1 vii
Why This Book Exists xi
A Note on the Title? What Women No About Men vii
David Selley – Guinnes World Record Attempt xiv

PART 1
   Chapter 1 – Kindness 3
   Chapter 2 – Honesty 11
   Chapter 3 – Passion 17
   Chapter 4 – Humor 23
   Chapter 5 – Attitude 29
   Chapter 6 – Personality 36
   Chapter 7 – Hygiene 41
   Chapter 8 – Spirituiality 47
   Chapter 9 – Finances 53
   Chapter 10 – Health 59
   Chapter 11 - Emotional Stability 65

PART 2 – Tools, Truth & Takeaways
   Chapter 12 – Tools That Make The Talk Easier 73
      Tool #1: The 95/5 Technique 74
      Tool #2: The Emotional Richter Scale 79
      A Word From David 85
   Chapter 13 – Final Scorecard & Reflections 87

Bonus: Rants, Notes & Final Thoughts 93

TABLE OF CONTENTS - *Continued*

Beyond the Book –
  Boundaries with Benefits –
    A Journal for Saying No without Losing
    Your Mind 93

David Selley – The Businessman 95
The PAPA SERIES – Other Series Titles Available 97
David's Quotes 100
David's Books 101
My Creed – Poem 104
About the Author 105
Contact David Selley 106

When Words Just Aren't Enough

All images in this book were created using AI and a good sense of humor. They're here purely for fun—to capture the spirit, the sass, and the occasional eyebrow raise that words just can't do alone. Nothing's too serious, everything's a little exaggerated, and every image is meant to make you smile (or snort-laugh). Enjoy the ride—one illustration at a tim

PART 1:

Chapter 1

"Kindness is love in action."

(And sometimes, it's just putting the toilet seat down without being asked.)

David Says
♥

Let me tell you something I've learned after 87 years of breathing the same air as millions of men:

- Kindness is never accidental -

It's either built into the way a man thinks...
...or it's something he's still Googling.

Now, I'm not talking about those big grand gestures that show up in romantic comedies.

I'm talking about the small, unsexy things:
—Like not interrupting you.
—Remembering what kind of tea you like.
—Or offering the last French fry even though he clearly wants it.

If a man can be kind when no one's watching, you've got yourself a rare species.

If he only shows kindness when he's guilty or wants something...Well, you've got a different kind of project on your hands.

What Kindness Looks Like
(*Real-Life Examples*)

 *Green Flag:*

He picks up your prescription when you're sick without asking what's in it.
("Yes, Dave... it's the one for cramps. Get over it.")

 Yellow Light:

He says he loves you but cuts you off during every sentence.
("Sure babe, go ahead... [immediately starts talking].")

 Red Flag:

He brings you flowers right after you catch him liking his ex's bikini pics on Instagram.
(Kindness shouldn't be damage control.)

No One Asked, But Here's My Opinion

"Kindness isn't about what he says—it's about how you feel when he's around. Safe? Seen? Or silently simmering with rage? You'll know."

Unofficial

No-O-Meter
How the Men in My Life Score

(A completely biased, emotionally-charged, snack-fueled ranking system)

We all know some men deserve statues... and some deserve *sticky notes* with "NOPE" written in red Sharpie. So I've created a handy little scoring system — based purely on real-life interactions, emotional survival, and snack-based appreciation — to help you determine how the men in your life measure up.

Name/Nickname	Score (1–10)	Quick Example or Story
Dad	9	Always brings me snacks when I'm sad.
Boyfriend	4	Gave me flowers... when he forgot my birthday.
Uncle Joe	7	Sends me good memes every morning.

Name/Nickname	Score (1–10)	Quick Example or Story
Husband	5	Thinks cleaning the kitchen means pushing crumbs to one side.
Brother	3	Still doesn't know my birthday but remembers every football stat.
Ex	1	Told me I "overthink everything." Bye.
Neighbor Bob	8	Shovels my driveway *and* returns my Tupperware.
Son	10	Said I'm his hero. He wins forever.

How to Score *Your* Guys — The Official NO-o-Meter Rating Scale

Before you fill out your chart, answer these pressing questions for each man in your life. Add up the points and tally the truth.

Ask yourself:
✓ Listens without interrupting? → **+2**
✓ Remembers your birthday *without Facebook*? → **+2**

- ✓ Does chores without being asked *and does them right?* → **+2**
- ✗ Said "You're overreacting" at least once? → **–2**
- ✗ Blamed the dog for something he clearly did? → **–1**
- ✓ Made you laugh when you wanted to cry? → **+2**
- ✓ Fixed something without YouTube? (honestly impressive) → **+1**
- ✗ Thinks Febreze = cleaning? → **–1**
- ✓ Brings snacks when you don't ask? (marry him) → **+1**

Score out of 10. No decimals. No do-overs. Petty is allowed.

Your Turn!
Fill in Your Personal NO-o-Meter

Name/Nickname	Score (1–10)	Quick Example or Story

(P.S. Showing them your answers is optional. Framing it on the fridge? That's on you.)

RED FLAG 🚩 RADAR:
Kindness Edition

Watch out for these signs of **fake kindness**:

iou and cookies

🚩 He only helps *after* a guilt trip.

🚩 Kind to strangers, cold at home.

🚩 Uses the word "sweetheart" like punctuation but never actually listens.

🚩 Keeps score: "Remember when I brought you soup that one time… in 2019?"

IF HE SCORES A 9 OR 10…
You lucky duck.
Celebrate him.
Buy him a burrito.
Or at least say thank you with more than just a emoji.

IF HE SCORES A 3 OR BELOW…
Consider using the **95/5 Method**
(see Chapter 11).
Or possibly a spiritual retreat. For *him*. Alone.
With no Wi-Fi.

YOUR NOTES, RANTS, OR PRAISE

Say what you REALLY think.
Praise him, roast him, write your next therapy session — no one's judging.

_____

_____

_____

_____

_____

_____

_____

_____

_____

_____

_____

_____

_____

_____

Chapter 2

"The truth always comes out… eventually"

(Especially when you leave your phone face-up on the table.)

WHAT HONESTY REALLY MEANS

Honesty in a relationship isn't just about whether he lies—it's about **how** he tells the truth.

Does he open up when it matters? Or only confess when he's caught?

Does he tell you what's *real*, even when it's uncomfortable? Or does he sugarcoat everything to avoid a reaction?

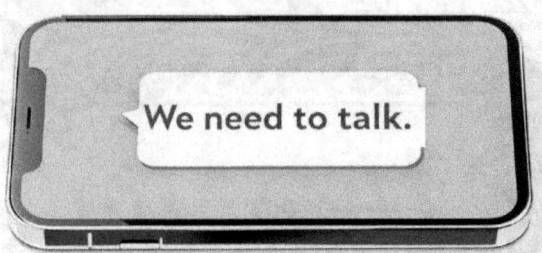

The truth always comes out – eventually.

Honesty is the foundation of trust—and without it, everything else is just... PR.

Whether it's about where he's been, how he feels, or why the Amazon package went missing *again*, honesty is the signal that you're on the same team (not playing emotional dodgeball).

David Says
♥

"A man who tells the truth even when it's inconvenient? Keep him.

A man who tells *part* of the truth, in a carefully rehearsed monologue?

Let's just say... that script's been workshopped before."

WHAT HONESTY LOOKS LIKE (REAL-LIFE EXAMPLES)

The truth always comes out – eventually.

 **Green Flag:**
He admits when he messed up, and doesn't blame Mercury in retrograde.

 **Yellow Light:**
He tells the truth... but only after three rounds of "Seriously, just be honest."

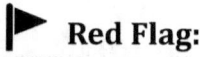 **Red Flag:**

"I DIDN'T LIE— I JUST DIDN'T TELL YOU."

BEEN THERE, SAID THAT:

"If you have to double-check his stories with Google and his mom, the trust ship may have sailed... and sunk."

No-O-Meter
Honesty EDITION

Scoring time! Give your guys a 1–10 based on how honest they are — not just when it's easy, but when it counts.

Name/Nickname	Score (1–10)	Quick Example or Story
Dad	9	Always told me the truth—even when I didn't want it. (Thanks, Dad.)
Boyfriend	3	"Forgot" to mention he still texts his ex.
Husband	6	Means well... but has a PhD in strategic phrasing.
Brother	8	Brutally honest. Emphasis on brutal.
Friend	10	Told me I had spinach in my teeth before the wedding photos.

Ask yourself...
- ✓ Owns his mistakes → **+2**
- ✓ Doesn't dodge questions → **+2**
- ✓ Admits when he forgot → **+1**
- ✓ Honest with money → **+2**
- ✓ Has nothing to hide on his phone → **+1**
- ✗ Says "I'm just trying to protect you" → **−2**
- ✗ Changes the subject when you ask direct questions → **−1**
- ✗ Guilts you for wanting honesty → **−2**
- ✗ "That's not what I meant" (after every disagreement) → **−1**

Add it up. Circle the score. Then sit with it.

IF HE SCORES A 9 OR 10...
Pop the champagne—or at least tell him "thank you" without a raised eyebrow.

You've got a rare one. Protect it.

IF HE SCORES A 3 OR BELOW...
Girl. Turn on "Detective Mode."
Or better yet—consider whether being confused all the time is your love language.

YOUR NOTES, RANTS, OR PRAISE
(The truth hurts, but lying hurts worse.)

Chapter 3

"Passion is energy made visible."

(And no, we're not just talking about what happens under the covers.)

WHAT PASSION REALLY MEANS

Passion in a relationship is more than steamy kisses and Saturday night fireworks (although, yes, those are appreciated).

Real passion is about how alive he is around you... and about life in general.

Is he excited to be with you?
Does he make you feel like you matter — or like you're the side project between football games and leftover meatloaf?

Passion is about presence.
About enthusiasm.
About *spark*.

(And not the kind you only see on vacation with good lighting and wine.)

David Says

♥

Listen—passion fades. That's normal.

But if you've been with a guy longer than a frozen pizza lasts, and you're already roommates with no eye contact... we may have a problem.

Passion isn't about performance. It's about **connection**. If he's more passionate about his fantasy football team than your actual reality?

He may be living in the wrong league.

WHAT PASSION LOOKS LIKE
(REAL-LIFE EXAMPLES)

🚩 **Green Flag:**

He kisses you like he means it — even when you're in sweatpants, holding a basket of laundry.

🚩 **Yellow Light:**

He says "I love you" out of habit, not heat. (Like he's punching a time card.)

🚩 **Red Flag:**

He only initiates affection after you threaten to cancel Netflix... or his credit card.

NO ONE ASKED, BUT HERE'S MY OPINION

Passion doesn't always mean drama.

But if you feel invisible in your own relationship — that's a red flag dressed as a beige bathrobe.

No-O-Meter
Passion EDITION
RATE YOUR MAN – PASSION

Name/Nickname	Score (1–10)	Quick Example or Story
Husband	6	Good hugs, but I'm starting to feel like his favorite hoodie.
Boyfriend	8	Still grabs my hand when we walk — and pulls me in close in public. 🖤
Ex	2	Thought "passion" was a cologne. Used it once. On our anniversary.
Crush	9	Makes me laugh *and* listen. He might be dangerous… in a good way. 😊

Ask yourself...
✓ Makes you feel wanted (not just needed) → +2

- ✓ Initiates affection
  (not just convenience cuddles) → **+2**
- ✓ Looks at you like he still sees *you* → **+1**
- ✓ Talks about the future with excitement → **+2**
- ✓ Still gets flirty sometimes → **+1**
- ✗ Needs reminders that foreplay is not just for birthdays → **−2**
- ✗ Compliments your outfit... then asks if it's new *every time* → **−1**
- ✗ Emotionally MIA unless it's game day → **−2**
- ✗ Says "passion fades" like it's a defense strategy → **−1**

Add it up. Sit with it. Dance it out if you need to.

IF HE SCORES A 9 OR 10...
You've got a rare spark — keep it lit.

Do something spontaneous and thank the relationship gods.

IF HE SCORES A 3 OR BELOW...
You deserve to be wanted, not just tolerated. Consider scheduling a talk... or a solo weekend getaway with better lighting.

YOUR NOTES, RANTS, OR PRAISE

*(Because sometimes passion shows up,
and sometimes it ghosts you.)*

Chapter 4

"If you can laugh together, you can last together."

(Unless his idea of humor is fart jokes at dinner... then we need to talk.)

WHAT HUMOR REALLY MEANS

Humor isn't just about being funny — it's about being able to **laugh through life together**.

It's how you both handle stress, awkward moments,

burned dinners, and the fact that he still can't load the dishwasher right.

A man with great humor:
- Doesn't take himself too seriously
- Can laugh *with* you, not just *at* things
- Knows when to lighten the mood — and when to zip it

Humor can get you through a lot.
Silence, tension, or forced laughter? Not so much.

David Says
♥

I've lived through wars, recessions, a teenage daughter, and the invention of TikTok.

Wanna know what kept me sane? **Laughter.**

If a man makes you laugh when you're angry — and doesn't make you angrier — keep him.

If he *is* the joke and doesn't know it… proceed with caution.

WHAT HUMOR LOOKS LIKE
(REAL-LIFE EXAMPLES)

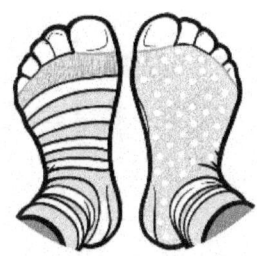

⚑ Green Flag:
He laughs at himself. Even when he wears mismatched socks to your mother's house.
(And then says, "I was testing her attention to detail.")

⚑ Yellow Light:
He repeats the same 3 dad jokes.
Daily. With confidence.
(*"Did I already say this one? Doesn't matter — it's gold."*)

⚑ Red Flag:
Thinks teasing you about your weight, your friends, or your dreams is "just a joke."

(It's not. It's a  in a clown nose.)

FROM THE GUY WHO'S SEEN IT ALL

"If he can't laugh during life's chaos, he'll probably yell instead.

Laughter is cheaper than therapy and twice as effective."

No-O-Meter

RATE YOUR MAN – *Humor*

Name/Nickname	Score (1–10)	Quick Example or Story
Husband	8	Makes me laugh-snort regularly. Once made the plumber laugh too.
Boyfriend	5	Sometimes funny, sometimes *tries* to be. We're working on it.
Ex	2	Made fun of my laugh. Big mistake. Huge.
Brother	9	Could do stand-up. Sometimes wish he would — just not at Thanksgiving.

Ask yourself...
✓ Makes you laugh even when you're mad → +2
✓ Laughs at himself (not just at you) → +2
✓ Knows when to lighten the mood → +2

✓ Can joke without being mean → +1
✓ Shares your sense of humor (or at least tries) → +1
✗ Thinks teasing you about sensitive stuff is "just being honest" → –2
✗ Uses humor to deflect real issues → –2
✗ Can't take a joke about himself → –1
✗ Laughs *at* you more than *with* you → –1

Add it up. Smile if you need to. Grimace if you have to. But be honest about the score.

YOUR NOTES, RANTS, OR PRAISE

*(Because sometimes passion shows up,
and sometimes it ghosts you.)*

Chapter 5

"A good attitude is contagious— unfortunately, so is a bad one."

(And if he enters every room like it owes him something... that's a clue.)

WHAT ATTITUDE REALLY MEANS

Attitude isn't what he *says*—it's the energy he brings into the room. Does he lift you up... or suck the life out of you like a joy-hungry vacuum?

A great attitude shows up in the little things:
- How he reacts when plans change
- Whether he complains or adapts
- If he encourages your goals—or competes with them

Attitude affects everything.

And bad attitude? Well… that stuff spreads faster than a cold at Christmas.

♥

Look, I've been around long enough to know:

- A man with a positive attitude can make a bad day better
- A man with a negative one can make a great life feel like a punishment.

If he's always the victim, the critic, or the storm cloud in every sunny moment...he might need a new script—or a mirror.

THAT ATTITUDE LOOKS LIKE (REAL-LIFE EXAMPLES)

🚩 **Green Flag:**
He shrugs off setbacks with a laugh and says, "We'll figure it out."

🚩 **Yellow Light:**
He handles life fine... until things don't go *his* way. Then cue the silent treatment.

🚩 **Red Flag:**
He treats every inconvenience like a personal attack. (*The coffee was lukewarm? Clearly, the world hates him.*)

STRAIGHT FROM THE MAN MANUAL (PAGE MISSING)

"Life's hard enough. Don't date someone who sees every glass as half empty... and blames you for spilling it."

No-O-Meter

RATE YOUR MAN – *Attitude*

Name/Nickname	Score (1–10)	Quick Example or Story
Husband	6	Usually upbeat, except when asked to call customer service.
Boyfriend	8	Turned a flat tire into a funny story. Helped a stranger while he was at it.
Ex	3	Eye-rolled his way through our entire relationship.
Neighbor Dan	9	Says hi to everyone, even the squirrels. Might run for mayor.

Ask Yourself
- ✓ Stays positive when things go sideways → +2
- ✓ Encouraging and supportive of your dreams → +2
- ✓ Doesn't take everything personally → +1
- ✓ Takes responsibility for his moods → +1
- ✓ Brings light, not drama → +2
- ✗ Wakes up mad and looks for a reason → –2

✘ Thinks sarcasm is a personality trait → –1
✘ Complains constantly... about everything → –2
✘ Acts like your joy is annoying → –1
✓ Add it up. Take a breath.

Adjust your own attitude if needed.

IF HE SCORES A 9 OR 10...

That's a *keeper* with emotional SPF built in. Enjoy the sunshine — it's rare.

IF HE SCORES A 3 OR BELOW...

Every day with him feels like walking on eggshells? Time to make an omelet and fly solo.

YOUR NOTES, RANTS, OR PRAISE
(Is he your hype man... or your emotional rain cloud?)

Chapter 6

"A positive personality is like sunshine—people feel it."

(And a negative one?
Feels like stepping in something… barefoot.)

WHAT PERSONALITY REALLY MEANS

A good personality doesn't mean he's the life of the party (though bonus points if he brings chips).

It means he's someone others enjoy being around—and *you* don't feel drained after five minutes of small talk.

A strong, positive personality is:
- Kind and curious
- Playful without being annoying
- Warm, funny, present, and real

The opposite? Sarcasm as a defense, mood swings as a personality trait, or just being… me.

David Says
♥

Look, not everyone needs to be the next Ryan Reynolds. But if his idea of "personality" is one-word answers, grunts, or just reposting memes—Houston, we have a boredom issue.

Good personality makes you feel comfortable. Bad personality makes you check your phone to fake an emergency.

WHAT PERSONALITY LOOKS LIKE (REAL-LIFE EXAMPLES)

▶ **Green Flag:**
He asks your waiter how their day is going—
and means it.

▶ **Yellow Flag:**
He's charming around new people...
but switches off at home.
(*"I'm just tired." Always tired.*)

▶ **Red Flag:**
Makes everything a debate, especially things like...
your feelings.

NO ONE ASKED, BUT HERE'S MY OPINION

A man's personality should light you up, not dim you down.

If you feel like you have to shrink to keep him comfortable, don't. Shrink him instead—*off your contact list.*

No-O-Meter

RATE YOUR MAN - *Personality*

Name/Nickname	Score (1–10)	Quick Example or Story
Husband	7	Kind to everyone, but oddly quiet around my family.
Boyfriend	9	Turns errands into adventures. Everyone loves him—even my grumpy neighbor.
Ex	3	Charming in public, grumpy in private. Like a personality magician.
Son	10	Funny, warm, curious. He got all the good genes.

Ask yourself
✓ Connects well with people → +2
✓ Warm, curious, and engaging → +2
✓ Makes life feel lighter, not heavier → +2

✓ Shows up with energy, not ego → **+1**
✓ Doesn't dominate conversations → **+1**
✗ Everything becomes about him → **−2**
✗ Gets annoyed when the attention's not on him → **−1**
✗ Drains your mood or vibe → **−2**
✗ Only "on" around certain people → **−1**

Add it up. Decide if you're vibing... or surviving.

IF HE SCORES A 9 OR 10...

That's a man who brings joy with him.
He's the spark. The glue. The good kind of weird.

IF HE SCORES A 3 OR BELOW...

You're not his audience.
And this show might need to close early.

YOUR NOTES, RANTS, OR PRAISE
*(Personality isn't everything...
unless he has none. Then it kinda is.)*

―――――――――――――――――――
―――――――――――――――――――
―――――――――――――――――――

Chapter 7

"If you can smell him before you see him—it's a no."

(And yes, "natural musk" is not a love language.)

WHAT *Hygiene* REALLY MEANS

Hygiene isn't just about grooming — it's about respect. Respect for his body, for shared space, for your nose, and honestly, for humanity.

Does he shower regularly?

Does he clip what needs clipping and scrub what needs scrubbing?

Or does his idea of freshening up involve spraying cologne over a bad decision?

Good hygiene says: "I care."

'If you can smell him before you see him—it's a no.'

David Says
♥

Back in my day, we didn't have a 12-step skincare routine. But we still bathed. With soap. Daily.

Hygiene isn't about perfection—it's about effort. And if he calls you high maintenance for not wanting to cuddle with a human hamper...that's not a red flag, that's a hazmat situation.

WHAT HYGIENE LOOKS LIKE
(REAL-LIFE EXAMPLES)

 Green Flag:
He smells great, trims his nails, flosses (!!!), and always has extra deodorant in his glove box.

 Yellow Light:
He's clean... when reminded. Repeatedly.
(*"Babe, did you shower today?" "Did I need to?"*)

 Red Flag:
He "doesn't believe" in soap.
Or sheets. Or toenail clippers.
Help.

JUST SAYIN'...

If you have to choose between loving him or sharing a bathroom with him... it might be time for separate sinks—or separate zip codes.

RATE YOUR MAN – *Hygiene*

Name/Nickname	Score (1–10)	Quick Example or Story
Husband	8	Clean, smells good, but still thinks beard trimmers are optional.
Boyfriend	5	Has potential. Just needs… coaching. Like, a lot.
Ex	2	Wore the same T-shirt for 3 days. I left. The shirt stayed.
Friend-Zoned Crush	9	Always polished. Too polished. Might be in love with his mirror.

Ask Yourself:
- ✓ Smells good (consistently) → +2
- ✓ Clean hair, skin, and clothes → +2
- ✓ Cares about grooming → +2
- ✓ Maintains shared spaces → +1

- ✓ Brings breath mints or floss → **+1**
- ✗ Has "laundry piles" that have become roommates → **−2**
- ✗ Needs reminders to brush his teeth → **−2**
- ✗ Smells like a gym bag but hasn't worked out → **−1**
- ✗ Calls wet wipes a "shower" → **−1**

Score it. Sniff test optional. Soap required.

IF HE SCORES A 9 OR 10...
Congratulations.
You found the holy grail: *Clean, conscious, and probably wrinkle-free.*

IF HE SCORES A 3 OR BELOW...
This isn't a man. This is a cleaning project disguised as a boyfriend.
(If you've ever lit a candle because of him... you're not alone.)

YOUR NOTES, RANTS, OR PRAISE
(If you've ever lit a candle because of him... you're not alone.)

Chapter 8

"A spiritual man listens with more than just his ears."

(And ideally, he doesn't just quote TikTok monks.)

WHAT Spirituality REALLY MEANS

Spirituality isn't about church attendance or crystal collections.

It's about depth, meaning, and whether he believes there's more to life than fast food and fantasy football.

A spiritual man doesn't need to be religious. He just needs to be rooted in something beyond his ego.
- Does he reflect before reacting?
- Seek peace instead of control?
- Live by values, not vibes?

Spirituality shows up in patience, kindness, humility... and in how he behaves when no one's keeping score.

David Says
♥

Let me be clear: spirituality isn't about being perfect. It's about being *present*—with yourself, your partner, and whatever higher power you believe in.

A spiritual man isn't preachy. He's peaceful. He knows when to sit in silence, when to offer comfort, and when to put his phone down and actually *listen*.

WHAT SPIRITUALITY LOOKS LIKE
(REAL-LIFE EXAMPLES)

🚩 **Green Flag:**
He meditates, prays, or journals without
making it a performance.
(And never judges what you believe.)

🚩 **Yellow Light:**
He says, "I'm spiritual, not religious,"
but can't explain what that means.
(*Spoiler: It's just something he heard on a podcast once.*)

🚩 **Red Flag:**
Thinks *he* is the higher power.

FROM THE GUY WHO'S SEEN IT ALL

"Spirituality isn't about incense and quotes.
It's about living with intention.

If he can't find meaning in anything—he may not bring much meaning to you either."

No-O-Meter

RATE YOUR MAN – *Spirituality*

Name/Nickname	Score (1–10)	Quick Example or Story
Husband	7	Prays quietly every night. Never brags about it. Solid human.
Boyfriend	4	Once went to a sound bath. Mostly for the snacks.
Ex	2	Said he was "enlightened," then ghosted me.
Friend	9	Reads, reflects, respects people. Might be Buddha in cargo shorts.

Ask yourself:

✓ Reflective, calm, grounded → +2
✓ Values growth, connection, purpose → +2
✓ Respects your beliefs (even if different) → +2
✓ Seeks peace, not control → +1

- ✓ Lives by values, not trends → **+1**
- ✗ Thinks "manifesting" means skipping responsibility → **−2**
- ✗ Only spiritual when it benefits him → **−2**
- ✗ Hasn't had a deep thought since 2007 → **−1**
- ✗ Uses "energy" as an excuse to cancel plans → **−1**

Score it. Light a candle. Say a prayer (if needed).

IF HE SCORES A 9 OR 10...
He's got soul. Celebrate that.
And maybe go to yoga with him once in a while.

IF HE SCORES A 3 OR BELOW...
Look, we all lose our way sometimes.
But if you're dating a spiritual tumbleweed...
it might be time to grow elsewhere.

YOUR NOTES, RANTS, OR PRAISE
(Because spiritual chemistry matters too.)

_____
_____
_____
_____
_____

Chapter 9

"A healthy man who can manage a budget is a rare gem."

(And if he can't... you might be dating
a very charming liability.)

WHAT *Finances* REALLY MEAN

Forget tall, dark, and handsome.

Try **hydrated, insured, and not emotionally allergic to budgeting**.

Finances are rarely romantic on the surface. But they are **relationship survival skills**.
- Can he take care of himself *and* contribute to a shared life?
- Does he know where his money goes—or where it disappears?
- Is he investing in his future… or just his video game setup?

It's not about six figures. It's about stability, responsibility, and long-term *livability*.

David Says
♥

You can be madly in love… but if he treats his bank account like Monopoly money, you're in for a ride.

I've learned the hard way—**love does not pay the electric bill**.

Money management isn't about being rich. It's about being **ready**.

Because a man who dodges financial responsibility will eventually dodge emotional responsibility, too.

WHAT FINANCIAL STABILITY LOOKS LIKE

🚩 **Green Flag:**
He has a budget and a plan. Even for fun stuff.

🚩 **Yellow Light:**
He's "working on it" but avoids certain topics like taxes, debt, or splitting the dinner bill.

🚩 **Red Flag:**
Thinks Venmo is a retirement strategy and cash apps are a love language.

NO ONE ASKED, BUT HERE'S MY OPINION

If you feel like his mother, his banker, and his backup plan—you're not in love. You're in customer service.

No-O-Meter
RATE YOUR MAN – *Finances*

Name/Nickname	Score (1–10)	Quick Example or Story
Husband	7	Budget spreadsheet, pays bills... still hates coupons.
Boyfriend	4	Pays rent late, but always has concert tickets.
Ex	1	Thought "credit score" was a type of video game.
Son	9	Budget-savvy, debt-free, and already investing. How did this happen?

Ask yourself
✓ Pays bills on time → **+2**
✓ Has savings (or a plan) → **+2**
✓ Talks honestly about money → **+2**
✓ Knows what "financial goals" mean → **+1**
✓ Understands credit and uses it wisely → **+1**

✘ Buys impulsively, regrets it loudly → –2
✘ Thinks planning is "boring" → –2
✘ Is cagey about money conversations → –1
✘ Thinks "I got this =no explanation ever → –1

Add it up. Your love story should
not include overdraft fees.

IF HE SCORES A 9 OR 10...

Financially secure *and* self-aware?
That's a rare combo—keep him and keep the receipts.

IF HE SCORES A 3 OR BELOW...

You might be falling for *potential*...
but your future deserves a partner, not a project.

YOUR NOTES, RANTS, OR PRAISE

*(Money talks... and yours should be
having better conversations.)*

Chapter 10

"He doesn't have to run marathons... but walking to the mailbox shouldn't wind him."

(And no, energy drinks don't count as wellness.)

WHAT *Health* REALLY MEANS

When we say "health," we're not talking about abs, apps, or avocado toast.

We're talking about whether he's **taking care of the body he's expecting you to live next to for the next 30 years**.

Health is more than how he looks.

It's how he lives. How he eats. How he sleeps. How he *deals* with stress.

- Does he care about being strong, clear-headed, and present?
- Does he move his body… or just complain about it?
- Is he investing in longevity—or just reacting when things break?

Healthy & Wealthy

You can't force someone to care about their health. But if they don't—you'll eventually be the one doing the caregiving.

David Says
♥

Trust me on this one: health sneaks up on you.

When you're young, you think you're invincible. Then suddenly you sneeze wrong and pull a muscle.

If he's ignoring his health now, he's **not just risking his future**—he's risking *yours* too.

WHAT *Health* LOOKS LIKE
(REAL-LIFE EXAMPLES)

🚩 **Green Flag:**
Drinks water, moves daily, eats food with colors that aren't just ketchup and cheese.

🚩 **Yellow Light:**
Used to be active. Now he's "taking a break"… that's lasted 8 months.

🚩 **Red Flag:**
Thinks sleep is for the weak, vegetables are a scam, and beer is hydration.

FROM THE GUY WHO'S SEEN IT ALL

"You can't date a man's potential health.

You date who he is—and what his habits are saying about where he's headed."

RATE YOUR MAN - *Health*

Name/Nickname	Score (1–10)	Quick Example or Story
Husband	7	Walks every morning, drinks tea, but *refuses* to eat anything green.
Boyfriend	5	Gym membership = yes. Uses it = questionable.

Name/Nickname	Score (1–10)	Quick Example or Story
Ex	2	Said walking to the fridge was cardio.
Brother	9	Meal preps, stretches, even reads food labels. We don't know who raised him.

Ask Yourself:
- ✔ Prioritizes regular checkups → **+2**
- ✔ Eats reasonably well → **+2**
- ✔ Moves his body regularly → **+2**
- ✔ Gets enough sleep → **+1**
- ✔ Open to mental health conversations → **+1**
- ✘ Thinks vitamins cancel out junk food → **–2**
- ✘ Avoids doctors out of ego or fear → **–2**
- ✘ Thinks hydration = soda → **–1**
- ✘ Laughs at the idea of stress management → **–1**

Score it honestly.
Then go drink some water together.

IF HE SCORES A 9 OR 10...
You've found a man who plans to stick around—
in good shape, and with energy to spare.
That's hot.

IF HE SCORES A 3 OR BELOW...
If he treats his health like an afterthought...
you might want to start thinking ahead—without him.

YOUR NOTES, RANTS, OR PRAISE
(Because "I'm fine" isn't a health plan.)

Chapter 11

"The real test is how he acts when things go wrong."

(And yes, throwing the remote over a slow Wi-Fi connection counts.)

WHY THIS IS THE +1 THAT CHANGES EVERYTHING

Because emotional stability is the secret ingredient no one writes on their wish list...

...until they've dated someone who has the emotional range of a confused blender.

EMOTIONAL ROLLERCOASTER   **EMOTIONAL STABILITY**

You can survive a bad joke, mismatched socks, even a little backseat driving.

But if he **melts down**, **shuts down**, or **explodes** every time life gets messy?

Girl, you're not in a relationship—you're riding a rollercoaster without a seatbelt.

This is the "quiet power" trait that makes all the others possible. Without it, even his good traits come with a warning label.

WHY THIS TRAIT MATTERS MOST
This is the one.
The trait that makes or breaks it all.

Because he can be funny, kind, passionate, even clean — but if he turns into a toddler with taxes or shuts down when you need him most... you're not in a relationship, you're in a *drama series*.

Emotional stability is **how he responds** to stress, disappointment, criticism, or vulnerability. It's not about being *stoic* — it's about being *steady*. Consistent Safe. Like a human emotional seatbelt.

You want passion? Great.
You want adventure? Wonderful.

But trust me, what you **need**—is a man who doesn't self-destruct every time life throws him a curveball.

Emotionally unstable men are charming on good days... and exhausting on the rest.

Find someone who doesn't just feel—but knows how to *handle* what he feels.

WHAT *Emotional Stability* LOOKS LIKE

▶ **Green Flag:**
He can disagree without disrespect. He breathes before reacting. He doesn't weaponize silence or volume.

▶ **Yellow Light:**
He handles conflict *okay*, but sometimes throws sarcasm or guilt in the ring.

▶ **Red Flag:**
Every disagreement = meltdown. He has 2 moods: "Fine" and "Why are you attacking me?"

STRAIGHT FROM THE MANUAL (THE *Emotional* EDITION)

If you're always walking on eggshells, eventually you'll forget how to dance.

RATE YOUR MAN

No-O-Meter
Emotional Stability EDITION

Name/Nickname	Score (1–10)	Quick Example or Story
Husband	8	Stays calm under pressure. Yelled once. Apologized before I even blinked. 🖤
Boyfriend	5	Mostly steady... but passive-aggressive texts are his love language.
Ex	2	Cried over burnt toast. Blamed me.
Crush	9	Level-headed, open, and emotionally fluent. Might be fictional.

Ask yourself
✓ Can handle conflict without blowing up → **+2**
✓ Stays calm when things go sideways → **+2**

- ✓ Apologizes when wrong → +2
- ✓ Validates your emotions → +1
- ✓ Can express his emotions → +1
- ✗ Gaslights or guilt-trips during conflict → –2
- ✗ Retreats, explodes, or sulks without talking → –2
- ✗ Blames you for everything → –1
- ✗ "I'm just emotional"=excuse for bad behavior –1

Add it up.
Then ask yourself: Does he regulate… or detonate?

IF HE SCORES A 9 OR 10…
That's not just a green flag—
it's a full-on **emotional spa day**.
Keep that man and treat him like the unicorn he is.

IF HE SCORES A 3 OR BELOW…
Love doesn't mean enduring chaos.
You're not his therapist, his punching bag, or his emotional assistant.

YOUR NOTES, RANTS, OR PRAISE
(Emotions are human. Stability is a gift.)

PART TWO:

Tools, Truths & Takeaways

Now that you've laughed, ranted, and rated... here's what to do with it all.

Chapter 12

"Because no one hands you a manual—so here's the next best thing."

Tool #1:
THE 95/5 TECHNIQUE

How to Quit Arguing About Absolute Rubbish and Actually Fix What Matters

Listen, if there's one thing I've learned after a lifetime of relationships (and a few furniture assembly fiascos), it's this:

        95% of the problem is pure nonsense.
    5% is where the truth—and the solution—live.

Let's break it down before you start another debate about who left the milk out.

The 95 %

The petty, pointless fluff that soaks up all your energy:
- The sigh he made when you asked for help.
- The tone of that "whatever."
- The fact that he can scroll on his phone for an hour but can't manage to answer your question.

These details are like glitter—annoying, everywhere, and not worth your sanity.

The 5%

The real, meaty stuff:
- You want to feel respected.
- You want to feel chosen.
- You want to know you matter more than whatever he's distracted by.

Most of the time, you're not mad about the crumbs on the counter. You're mad about feeling invisible.

My Personal Example
(So You Don't Feel Alone)

Sonja and I once nearly called the divorce lawyer over wallpaper. Yes—WALLPAPER.

I thought eyeballing the alignment was perfectly reasonable. She thought I was a lunatic.

We argued until the glue dried—and the real issue had nothing to do with crooked stripes.

The 95%: The wallpaper looked like a toddler hung it.
The 5%: We both wanted to feel like we were working together and listening to each other.

How to Use the 95/5 Technique
(Before You Lose Your Mind)

1. Pause.
   Seriously. Take a breath. This is where most people fail—they react instead of thinking.
2. Ask Yourself:
   "What's the real 5% here?"
   If your brain answers, *"Because he's an idiot,"* try again. That's still the 95%.
3. Zoom In.
   Focus on the emotional need behind the mess.
4. Speak to the Heart of It.
   Be clear, be kind, and skip the sarcasm—unless you're both in the mood to laugh about it.

Quick Activity
(If You're Brave)

- Think of a recent argument that made you wonder if you should move to a remote island.
- Write down what it *seemed* to be about (the 95%).
- Then, write what it was *really* about (the 5%).
- Ask yourself: *How would this have played out if we'd focused on the 5%?*

When to Pull This Out of Your Toolkit

Dating?
Use it early, before you start collecting resentments.

Living together?

Apply it weekly—because life is full of irritating details. Decades in?

This is how you keep liking each other after the honeymoon phase is ancient history.

Remember this:

You can either be right about the 95% or be happy about the 5%.
Pick wisely.

Tool #2:
THE EMOTIONAL RICHTER SCALE
"Use numbers, not yelling."

Emotions get loud. And misunderstood.

You say, *"I'm upset."*
He hears: *"You're attacking me."*

You say, *"I'm fine."*
He hears: *"Cool, I'll go play Xbox."*

> Let's translate feelings into something he *actually* understands: numbers.

How it works:
You assign a **number (1–10)**
to how strongly you're feeling.
Then say:
"This is an 8.5 for me emotionally. Can you see how important it is?"

Boom. Instant clarity. Instant shift.

Number	What It Means
1–2	Mild annoyance. Easily resolved.
3–4	Frustration. Needs a convo.

Number	What It Means
5–6	Hurt feelings. Take seriously.
7–8	High emotional impact. Needs full attention.
9–10	Critical. Non-negotiable. This is deep.

Why it works:

- Bypasses emotional confusion
- Sets the tone for empathy, not defense
- Helps both people gauge urgency without guessing

TRY THIS PHRASE:

"This isn't a casual issue. It's a 9 on my emotional scale. I need you to hear me fully."

The Emotional Richter Scale

Because Some Fights Are Just Tiny Tremors (and Others Are Total Disasters).

Listen—relationships don't just have *ups and downs*. They have *seismic events*.

Sometimes it's a 1.0: you roll your eyes, you move on. Other times? Full 9.0 meltdown, lasting aftershocks, and someone's definitely sleeping on the couch. Emotions are dramatic like that.

Here's my *completely scientific* (not really) tool to help you figure out how serious this "problem" actually is—

so you can stop making Category 10 drama out of a Category 2 issue. Strap on your emotional hard hat and see where you land:

Magnitude 1.0 - 2.0
The Mildly Annoying Discovery
- He leaves every cabinet door open like poltergeists live there.
- You shut them. Repeatedly.
- Annoying? Yes. Divorce-worthy? Not yet.

Magnitude 2.1 - 3.0
The Shopping Styles Clash
- You go in with a list.
- He treats it like a treasure hunt for things you don't need.
- You wonder if he's ever heard of a budget.

Magnitude 3.1 - 4.0
The "I Thought You Knew" Moment
- Who was supposed to book the dinner? Pay the bill? Feed the dog?
- Apparently, neither of you.
- Cue finger-pointing and exasperated sighs.

Magnitude 4.1 - 5.0
The Towel-Folding Standoff
- You grew up folding them like a hotel.
- He folds them like an angry toddler.
- Lines are drawn.

Magnitude 5.1 - 6.0
The Thermostat War Begins
- You want tropical comfort.
- He wants to feel like he's camping in the Arctic.
- No one wins except the utility company.

Magnitude 6.1 - 7.0
The "Just Drop It" Argument
- Starts minor.
- Ends with both of you staring silently out the car window like you're in an indie drama.

Magnitude 7.1 - 8.0
The Surprise Big Purchase
- He comes home with a giant TV, gaming system, or puppy.
- Your reaction: "So... we don't talk about these things first?"

Magnitude 8.1 - 9.0
The Couch Exile
- You're not even sure what started it.
- Neither of you will back down.
- Hope you like firm cushions.

Magnitude 9.1 - 10.0
The "What Were We Thinking?" Meltdown
- For a solid hour you both wonder if combining your lives was a brilliant plan or an ongoing social experiment.
- Usually passes. But you'll remember it.

David's Note:
"Here's the secret no one tells you: most of these quakes aren't about *what* you're fighting about. It's about *how* you're handling it.

The goal isn't to avoid tremors—they're part of the deal. The goal is to recognize when you're overreacting and calm the hell down before you crack the foundation."

Quick Tip:
When you feel a 7.0 coming on, ask yourself:
"Is this about the actual problem, or about me needing to be right?"

Surprising how often that little question can drop the scale to a 2.0.

Final Thought:
Love isn't earthquake-proof. But if you're both willing to reinforce the foundation—and laugh at your own drama once in a while—you'll survive the big ones just fine.

A Word from David

"Every woman I know has a list—tall, funny, employed, knows how soap works. But the smart ones? They learned to revise it.

You deserve laughter, honesty, peace, and a man who doesn't make you consult a group chat titled 'Avoid This One.'

And if you haven't found him yet? Maybe you're too busy becoming the kind of woman who doesn't settle for nonsense.

Look, most people spend years arguing about absolute rubbish and wondering why nothing changes. Don't be most people.

You can't control every emotion (trust me, I've tried). But you *can* control whether you react like an adult... or like you're auditioning for a reality show.

These tools won't fix everything. But they might just save you from another 2 a.m. text fight, an expensive therapy bill, or the joy of buying a second couch because someone slept too hard on the first.

Use them well. Laugh when you can. Apologize when

you should. And save your energy for the good stuff—like actually liking each other.

With respect, a wink, and the firm belief you deserve better than 'fine,' —David"

Chapter 13

"Time to tally the truth— and maybe text your therapist."

(Or your bestie. Or your group chat titled *'Avoid This One'*.)

YOUR TOP 3 MEN

Fill in your highest-scoring guys from the NO-o-Meter charts. Then decide what category they fall into: *Keeper, Maybe,* or *Nope.*

Name/Nickname	Total Score (Out of 110)	Verdict
		☐ Keeper ☐ Maybe ☐ Nope
		☐ Keeper ☐ Maybe ☐ Nope
		☐ Keeper ☐ Maybe ☐ Nope

WHAT I LEARNED

I want more of:

_____

_____

_____

_____

_____

I'm done tolerating:

I thought I wanted

...but I actually need

My emotional Richter scale will now include:

BONUS

RANTS, NOTES & FINAL THOUGHTS

Say What You REALLY Wanted to Say
(But Didn't)

This space is for everything you couldn't say out loud, didn't want to text, or aren't quite ready to post on social media. Rant, reflect, or write your next therapy session. It's your page now.

Ready to Go Beyond the Book?

BOUNDARIES WITH BENEFITS
A Journal for Saying No Without Losing Your Mind

Turn reading into *real results* **with Boundaries with Benefits**—your personal space to get honest, get clear, and finally say *NO* without losing your mind (or your sense of humor).

- **Expanded NO-O-Meter pages** to score every man in your life (no mercy needed).
- **Deep-dive prompts** to uncover what you really want (and why you deserve it).

- **Space for uncensored rants, sticky-note truths**, and writing the messages you'll never send.
- **Reflection sections** to spot patterns, red flags, and your role in the chaos.
- **Fun extras** for Girls' Nights, bridal showers, or wine-soaked therapy with friends.
- **Room to plan** your non-negotiables, relationship goals, and future "NOs."

What will you get out of it?

Clarity. Confidence. Better boundaries.
And a hilarious, honest map of what (and who) you want to say *YES* to next.

Grab your copy—
because reading is good, but writing your truth changes everything.

The Businessman and Entrepreneur in the USA

David Selley's PAPA Book Series: A Guinness World Record Journey

David Selley's **PAPA Book Series** is more than a collection of stories—it's a testament to a life well-lived, spanning three continents and over eight decades of experiences in family, business, and personal growth. As part of his **Guinness World Record attempt to become the oldest author to publish the most books in one year**, this series captures the wisdom, resilience, and entrepreneurial spirit that have defined his journey.

From his tough childhood in England to his transformative years in Canada, and his entrepreneurial success in the USA, David's books weave together memoir, business insights, and life lessons. At the heart of the series is his 65-year marriage, a remarkable testament to love, perseverance, and partnership.

Beyond personal storytelling, David's latest entrepreneurial venture, the International Entrepreneur Association (IEA), introduces readers to a new vision for global business networking. By connecting importers and exporters in a streamlined system, David aims to create new opportunities for businesses worldwide.

SERIES TITLES AVAILABLE NOW:

(*Includes books newly released or publishing soon*)

PAPA #1: The Boy in England and Growing Up Tough is a tale of resilience and survival from David's early days in England.

PAPA #2: The Young Man in Canada provides a look at his transformative years in Canada, filled with personal and professional growth.

PAPA #3: The Businessman and Entrepreneur in the USA chronicles David's entry into the business world and his entrepreneurial adventures in the United States.

PAPA #4: The Entrepreneur: PAPAS Secret #4 takes a deep dive into his entrepreneurial mindset and the lessons learned from building businesses.

SERIES TITLES *(continued)*

PAPA #5: Three Lives, Three Lands
A condensed journey through David Selley's life in England, Canada, and the USA

PAPA #6: Married – The Four Seasons of Marriage reflects on the evolving phases of marriage over 65+ years, from spring to winter.

PAPA #7: How Is Your Relationship?
(How to Stay Married 65+ Years)

PAPA #8: The Father explores David's journey as a father, filled with challenges, love, and important lessons.

PAPA #9: The Grandfather – Leaving a Legacy is a heartwarming tribute to family and the importance of passing down wisdom and values.

PAPA #10: Health, Wealth & Happiness
(You Can Have All Three)
is a guide to achieving balance and abundance in life.

PAPA #11: The Investor – Nothing Down Real Estate... Yes! It Works presents proven strategies for real estate investing without upfront costs.

SERIES TITLES *(continued)*

PAPA #12: The Famous 50 Book Series is an exciting global vanity publishing project, connecting famous people across industries at *www.famous50.com*.

PAPA #13: GenMar – The Generational Marketing Advantage reveals how understanding generational values can transform marketing and deepen customer connection.

Papa #14 – What Women NO About Men
A witty, honest look at the ten traits women want in a man (plus one that changes everything), helping readers spot red flags and laugh along the way.

Papa #15 – BOUNDARIES WITH BENEFITS
A practical, cheeky journal for women to get clear on their "NOs," build better boundaries, and protect their peace with humor and heart.

Mindset
"You can IF you think you can." – Zig Ziglar

Leadership
*"Ask not what your country can do for you...
but what you can do for your country." – John F. Kennedy*

Personal Development
*"Change your thoughts and you change your world."
– Norman Vincent Peale*

Integrity
*"Try not to become a man of success.
Rather become a man of value." – Albert Einstein*

Self-Belief
*"Whatever the mind can conceive and believe,
it can achieve." – Napoleon Hill*

Innovation
*"The best way to predict the future
is to create it." – Peter F. Drucker*

Critical Thinking
*"People with polarized opinions will only educate
themselves to their level of ignorance." – David Selley*

Practical Wisdom
*"Never take advice from someone who has not
done what they are talking about." -- David Selley*

"How to Win Friends and Influence People"
by Dale Carnegie

"The Magic of Thinking Big"
by David J. Schwartz

"Think and Grow Rich"
by Napoleon Hill

"The Power of Positive Thinking"
by Norman Vincent Peale

"The Power of Focus"
by Jack Canfield, Mark Victor Hansen, and Les Hewitt

David's Favorite Books - *Continued*

"The Aladdin Factor"
by Jack Canfield and Mark Victor Hansen

"Innovation and Entrepreneurship"
by Peter F. Drucker

"Secrets of Power Negotiating"
by Roger Dawson

"See You at the Top"
by Zig Ziglar

"Live Your Dreams"
by Les Brown

The Art of Exceptional Living"
by Jim Rohn

**"Maximum Achievement:
Strategies and Skills That Will Unlock
Your Hidden Powers"**
by Brian Tracy

"The 21 Irrefutable Laws of Leadership"
by John C. Maxwell

My Creed
By Dean Alfange

*A powerful declaration of
self-reliance, entrepreneurship and personal freedom.*

I do not choose to be a common man,
It is my right to be uncommon ... if I can,
I seek opportunity ... not security.
I do not wish to be a kept citizen.
Humbled and dulled by having the
State look after me.
I want to take the calculated risk;
To dream and to build.
To fail and to succeed.
I refuse to barter incentive for a dole;
I prefer the challenges of life
To the guaranteed existence;
The thrill of fulfillment
To the stale calm of Utopia.
I will not trade freedom for beneficence
Nor my dignity for a handout
I will never cower before any master
Nor bend to any threat.
It is my heritage to stand erect.
Proud and unafraid;
To think and act for myself,
To enjoy the benefit of my creations
And to face the world boldly and say:
This, with God's help, I have done.

*All this is what it means to be an
"Entrepreneur."*

About the Author

David Selley

David Selley is an 87-year-old author, entrepreneur, and enthusiastic truth-teller with a knack for saying what most people only *think*. With a lifetime of personal stories, relationship lessons, and cheeky humor, David writes books that are part guide, part reality check, and always from the heart.

He's the author of ***Married Forever: The Four Seasons of Marriage***, a warm and honest look at long-term love inspired by his own 65+ year marriage. Known for his clarity, candor, and the occasional raised eyebrow, David's voice has struck a chord with readers who want the truth—served with a side of humor.

This book, *What Women NO About Men*, is one of several titles he's writing as part of his quest to break a **Guinness World Record**—to become the oldest man to publish the most books in a single year. (Yes, he's still competitive.)

He continues to write, mentor, and quietly marvel at how little some men understand women—and how much better things get when they finally do.

You can find more of his books, tools, and rants at: **www.IEA777.com**

Contact David Selley

www.iea777.com

davidselley08@gmail.com

1-800-388-3102